The Responsorial Psalter

Year B

Edited by Stephen Dean

McCRIMMONS
Great Wakering, Essex

First published 1987 by McCrimmon Publishing Co,
10–12 High Street, Great Wakering, Essex, SS3 0EQ.

Acknowledgements of the music settings will be found on page 80.

ISBN 0 85597 407 9

Cover design by Paul Shuttleworth
Music artwork by Sheila Mullen and Catherine Christmas
Typesetting by Fleetlines, Southend-on-Sea, Essex
Printed by Mayhew-McCrimmon Printers, Great Wakering, Essex

CONTENTS

FIRST SUNDAY OF ADVENT

Ps 79(80): 2-3. 15-16. 18-19   R.v.4

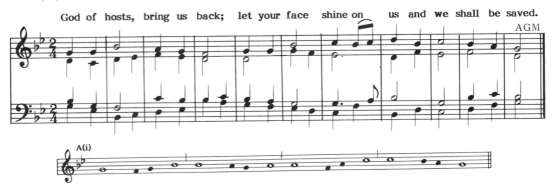

1 O shépherd of Ísrael, héar us,
   shine fórth from your chérubim thróne.
   O Lórd, róuse up your míght,
   O Lórd, cóme to our hélp.

2 God of hósts, turn agáin, we implóre,
   look dówn from héaven and sée.
   Vísit this víne and protéct it,
   the víne your right hánd has plánted.

3 May your hánd be on the mán you have chósen,
   the mán you have gíven your stréngth.
   And we shall néver forsáke you agáin:
   give us lífe that we may cáll upon your náme.

Gospel Acclamation   *Psalm 84(85): 8*

Let us see, O Lord, your mercy
and give us your saving help.

SECOND SUNDAY OF ADVENT

Ps 84(85): 9-10. 11-12. 13-14   *R.v.8*

1 I will hear what the Lord God <u>has</u> to say,
   a voice that speaks of peace,/
      peace <u>for</u> his people.
   His help is near for <u>those</u> who fear him
   and his glory will dwell <u>in</u> our land.

2 Mercy and faithful<u>ness</u> have met;
   justice and peace <u>have</u> embraced.
   Faithfulness shall spring <u>from</u> the earth
   and justice look <u>down</u> from heaven.

3 The Lord will <u>make</u> us prosper
   and our earth shall <u>yield</u> its fruit.
   Justice shall m<u>arch</u> before him
   and peace shall fol<u>low</u> his steps.

An alternative setting may be found on page 56.

Gospel Acclamation   *Luke 3:4.6*

Prepare a way for the Lord, make <u>his</u> paths straight,
and all mankind shall see the salva<u>tion</u> of God.

THIRD SUNDAY OF ADVENT

Luke 1: 46-48. 49-50. 53-54.   *R. Isaiah 61:10*

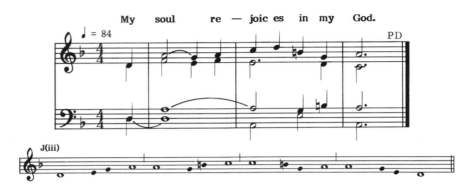

1   My soul glorifies the Lord,
    my spirit rejoices in God, my Saviour.
    He looks on his servant in her nothingness,
    henceforth all ages will call me blessed.

2   The Almighty works marvels for me.
    Holy his name!
    His mercy is from age to age,
    on those who fear him.

3   He fills the starving with good things,
    sends the rich away empty.
    He protects Israel, his servant,
    remembering his mercy.

Gospel Acclamation   *Luke 4:18*

The spirit of the Lord has been given to me.
He has sent me to bring good news to the poor.

FOURTH SUNDAY OF ADVENT

Ps 88(89): 2-3. 4-5. 27, 29.   *R.v.2*

1   I will sing for ever of your <u>love</u>, O Lord;
     through all ages my mouth will pro<u>claim</u> your truth.
     Of this I am sure, that your love <u>lasts</u> for ever,
     that your truth is firmly established <u>as</u> the heavens.

2   Happy the people who acclaim <u>such</u> a king,
     who walk, O Lord, in the light <u>of</u> your face,
     who find their joy every day <u>in</u> your name,
     who make your justice the source <u>of</u> their bliss.

3   For it is you, O Lord, who are the glory <u>of</u> their strength;
     it is by your favour that our might <u>is</u> exalted:
     for our ruler is in the keeping <u>of</u> the Lord;
     our king is in the keeping of the Holy <u>One</u> of Israel.

Psalm tone as above.

Gospel Acclamation   *Luke 1:38*

I am the handmaid <u>of</u> the Lord:
let what you have said be <u>done</u> to me.

CHRISTMAS

Midnight Mass

Ps 95(96): 1-2a. 2b-3. 11-13b. 13cd.   *R. Luke 2:11*

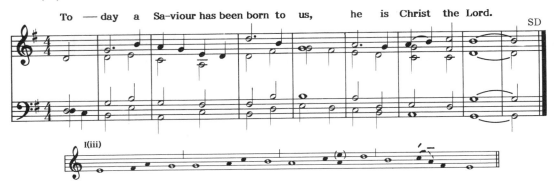

1 O sing a new song <u>to</u> the Lord,
   sing to the Lord <u>all</u> the earth.   *(omit c)*
   O sing to the Lórd, <u>bless</u> his name.

2 Proclaim his help <u>day</u> by day,
   tell among the na<u>tions</u> his glory   *(omit c)*
   and his wonders amóng <u>all</u> the peoples.

3 Let the heavens rejoice and earth be glad,/
      let the sea and all within it <u>thunder</u> praise,
   let the land and all it <u>bears</u> rejoice,
   all the trees of the wood shout for joy/
      at the presence of the Lord <u>for</u> he comes,
   he comes to <u>rúle</u> the earth.

4 With justice he will <u>rule</u> the world,   *(omit b + c)*
   he will judge the péoplés <u>with</u> his truth.

Psalm tone as above.

Gospel Acclamation   *Luke 2:10-11*

I bring you news <u>of</u> great joy:
today a saviour has been born to us, <u>Christ</u> the Lord.

Mass During the Day

Ps 97(98): 1.2-3b. 3c-4. 5-6.   *R.v.3*

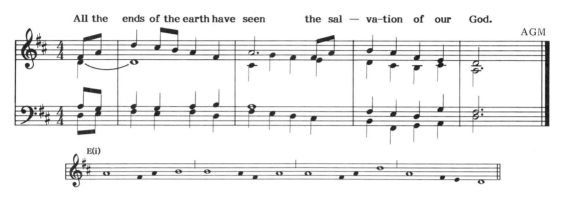

1 Sing a new song <u>to</u> the Lord
   for he <u>has</u> worked wonders.
   His right hand and his <u>ho</u>ly arm
   have <u>brought</u> salvation.

2 The Lord has made known <u>his</u> salvation;
   has shown his justice <u>to</u> the nations.
   He has remembered his <u>truth</u> and love
   for the <u>house</u> of Israel.

3 All the ends of the <u>earth</u> have seen
   the salvation <u>of</u> our God.
   Shout to the Lord <u>all</u> the earth,
   ring <u>out</u> your joy.

4 Sing psalms to the Lord <u>with</u> the harp,
   with the <u>sound</u> of music.
   With trumpets and the sound <u>of</u> the horn
   acclaim the <u>King</u>, the Lord.

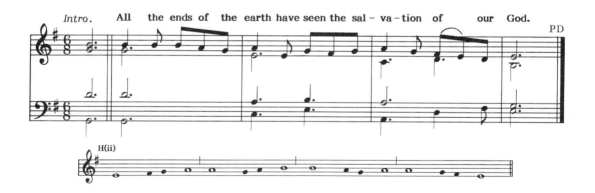

Gospel Acclamation

A hallowed day has dawned upon us./
   Come, you nations, worship the Lord,
for today a great light has <u>shone</u> down up<u>on</u> the earth.

THE HOLY FAMILY

When Year A readings are used   *Ps 127(128): 1-2. 3. 4-5.   R.cf.v.1*

1 O blessed are those who <u>fear</u> the Lord
and walk <u>in</u> his ways!
By the labour of your hands <u>you</u> shall eat.
You will be happy and prosp<u>er</u>.

2 Your wife like a <u>fruit</u>ful vine
in the heart <u>of</u> your house;
your children like shoots <u>of</u> the olive,
a<u>round</u> your table.

3 Indeed thus <u>shall</u> be blessed
the man who <u>fears</u> the Lord.
May the Lord bless <u>you</u> from Zion
all the days <u>of</u> your l<u>ife</u>!

Gospel Acclamation

May the peace of Christ reign <u>in</u> your hearts;
let the message of Christ find a <u>home</u> with you.

Alternative Setting for Year B (ad libitum)   Ps 104(105): 1-2. 3-4. 5-6. 8-9.   R.vv.7-8

1 Give thanks to the Lord, <u>tell</u> his name,
make known his deeds a<u>mong</u> the peoples.
O sing to him, <u>sing</u> his praise;
tell all his won<u>der</u>ful works!

2 Be proud of his <u>holy</u> name,
let the hearts that seek the <u>Lord</u> rejoice.
Consider the Lord <u>and</u> his strength;
constantly <u>seek</u> his face.

3 Remember the wonders <u>he</u> has done,
his miracles, the judge<u>ments</u> he spoke.
O children of Abraham, his servant,
O sons of the Ja<u>cob</u> he chose.

4 He remembers his cove<u>nant</u> for ever,
his promise for a thousand <u>gene</u>rations,
the covenant he <u>made</u> with Abraham,
the oath he <u>swore</u> to Isaac.

Gospel Acclamation   *see Mary, Mother of God*

SOLEMNITY OF MARY, MOTHER OF GOD

Ps 66(67): 2-3. 5. 6, 8.   *R.v.2*

1 God, be gracious and bless us
   and let your face shed its light upon us.
   So will your ways be known upon earth.
   and all nations learn your saving help.

2 Let the nations be glad and exult
   for you rule the world with justice.
   With fairness you rule the peoples,
   you guide the nations on earth.

3 Let the peoples praise you, O God;
   let all the peoples praise you.
   May God still give us his blessing
   till the ends of the earth revere him.

Gospel Acclamation

Hebrews 1:1-2

At various times in the past/
   and in various different ways
God spoke to our ancestors through the prophets;
* but in our own time, the last days,
he has spoken to us through his Son.

* *repeat chant*

SECOND SUNDAY AFTER CHRISTMAS

Ps 147:12-13. 14-15. 19-20.   *R. John 1:14*

The Word was made flesh, and lived a — mong us.

FO'C

1   O praise the <u>Lord</u>, Jerusalem!
    Zion, <u>praise</u> your God!
    He has strengthened the bars <u>of</u> your gates
    he has blessed the chil<u>dren</u> within you.

2   He established peace <u>on</u> your borders,
    he feeds you with <u>fin</u>est wheat.
    He sends out his word <u>to</u> the earth
    and swiftly runs <u>his</u> command.

3   He makes his word <u>known</u> to Jacob,
    to Israel his laws <u>and</u> decrees
    He has now dealt thus with <u>other</u> nations;
    he has not taught them <u>his</u> decrees.

The Word was made flesh and lived a — mong us.

MH

Gospel Acclamation   *cf. 1 Tim 3:16*

Glory be to you, O Christ, proclaimed <u>to</u> the pagans;
Glory be to you, O Christ, believed in <u>by</u> the world.

THE EPIPHANY OF THE LORD

Ps 71(72):1-2. 7-8. 10-11. 12-13.   R.cf.v.11

1. O God, give your judgement to the king,
   to a king's son your justice,
   that he may judge your people in justice
   and your poor in right judgement.

2. In his days justice shall flourish
   and peace till the moon fails.
   He shall rule from sea to sea,
   from the Great River to earth's bounds.

3. The kings of Tarshish and the sea coasts/
   shall pay him tribute.
   The kings of Sheba and Seba/
   shall bring him gifts.
   Before him all kings shall fall prostrate
   all nations shall serve him.

4. For he shall save the poor when they cry
   and the needy who are helpless.
   He will have pity on the weak
   and save the lives of the poor.

Gospel Acclamation   *Matthew 2:2*

We saw his star as it rose
and have come to do the Lord homage.

THE BAPTISM OF THE LORD

When Year A readings are used   Ps 28(29): 1-2. 3-4. 10-11.

The Lord will bless his peo-ple with peace.

1 O give the Lord, you <u>sons</u> of God,
   give the Lord <u>glory</u> and power;
   give the Lord the <u>glory of</u> his name.
   Adore the Lord in his <u>ho</u>ly court.

2 The Lord's voice resounding <u>on</u> the waters,
   the Lord on the immensity of waters;
   the voice of the Lord, <u>full</u> of power,
   the voice of the Lord, <u>full</u> of splendour.

3 The God of <u>glory</u> thunders.
   In his temple they <u>all</u> cry: 'Glory!'
   The Lord sat enthroned <u>over</u> the flood;
   The Lord sits as <u>king</u> for ever.

Gospel Acclamation   *Mark 9:8*

The heavens opened and the Father's <u>voice</u> resounded:
'This is my son, the beloved. <u>Lis</u>ten to him.'

Alternative Setting for Year B (ad libitum)   *Isaiah 12: 2-3. 4. 5-6.*   *R.v.3*

With joy you will draw wa - ter from the wells of sal — va — tion.

1 Truly God is my salvation,/
   I trust, I <u>shall</u> not fear.
   For the Lord is my <u>strength</u>, my song,
   he be<u>came</u> my saviour.
   With joy you will draw water/
   from the wells <u>of</u> salvation.

2 Give thanks to the Lord, give praise <u>to</u> his name!
   make his mighty deeds known <u>to</u> the peoples, *(omit C)*
   declare the greatness <u>of</u> his name.

3 Sing a psalm to the Lord/
   for he has done <u>glor</u>ious deeds,
   make them known to <u>all</u> the earth!
   People of Zion, sing and <u>shout</u> for joy
   for great in your midst is the Holy <u>One</u> of Israel.

for another setting see after the Fifth
Reading at the Easter Vigil, p.29

Gospel Acclamation
cf. John 1:29

John saw Jesus coming towards <u>him</u> and said:
This is the Lamb of God who takes away the sin <u>of</u> the world.

ASH WEDNESDAY

Ps 50(51): 3-4. 5-6. 12-13. 14, 17.   R.v.3

Have mer–cy on us, Lord, for we have sinned.

AGM

A(i)

1   Have mercy on me, God, in your kindness.
    In your compassion blot out my offence.
    O wash me more and more from my guilt
    and cleanse me from my sin.

2   My offences truly I know them;
    my sin is always before me.
    Against you, you alone, have I sinned;
    what is evil in your sight I have done.

3   A pure heart create for me, O God,
    put a steadfast spirit within me.
    Do not cast me away from your presence,
    nor deprive me of your holy spirit.

4   Give me again the joy of your help;
    with a spirit of fervour sustain me,
    O Lord, open my lips
    and my mouth shall declare your praise.

Have mer–cy on us, Lord, for we have sinned.

SD

J(i)

Gospel Acclamation

A pure heart create for me, O God,   *Ps 50(51):12, 14*
and give me again the joy of your help.
  or
Harden not your hearts today,   *Ps 94(95):8*
but listen to the voice of the Lord.

FIRST SUNDAY OF LENT

Ps 24(25): 4-5. 6-7. 8-9.   R.cf.v.10

1 Lórd, make me knów your wáys.
  Lórd, téach me your páths.
  Make me wálk in your trúth and téach me:
  for yóu are Gód my sáviour.

2 Remémber your mércy, Lórd,
  and the lóve you have shówn from of óld.
  In your lóve remémber mé,
  becáuse of your góodness, O Lórd.

3 The Lórd is góod and úpright.
  He shows the páth to thóse who stráy,
  he gúides the humble ín the ríght path;
  he téaches his wáy to the póor.

Psalm tone as above.

Gospel Acclamation   *Matthew 4:4*

Man does not live on bread alone,
but on every word that comes from the mouth of God.

SECOND SUNDAY OF LENT

Ps 115(116): 10,15. 16-17. 18-19.   R.Ps 114(116):9

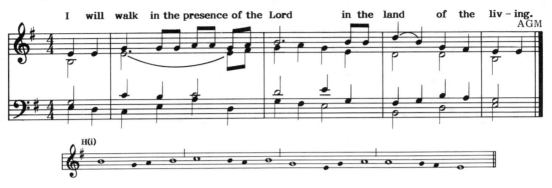

1 I trústed, éven <u>when</u> I sáid:
   'I am sórely afflícted.'
   O précious in the éyes <u>of</u> the Lórd
   is the déath <u>óf</u> his fáithful.

2 Your sérvant, Lord, your sérv<u>ant</u> am Í
   you have loó<u>sened</u> my bónds.
   A thánksgiving sácrif<u>ice</u> I máke:
   I will cáll on <u>the</u> Lórd's náme.

3 My vóws to the Lórd I <u>will</u> fulfíl
   befóre <u>all</u> his péople,
   in the cóurts of the hóuse <u>of</u> the Lórd,
   in your mídst, <u>Ó</u> Jerúsalem.

Gospel Acclamation   *Matthew 17:5*

From the bright cloud the Father's <u>voice</u> was heard:
'This is my Son, the Beloved. <u>Lis</u>ten to him.'

THIRD SUNDAY OF LENT

*The Readings for Year A may be used as alternatives. The Psalm for Year A is
Ps 94(95), as on the Fourth Sunday in Ordinary Time.*

Ps 18(19): 8. 9. 10. 11.   R. John 6:68

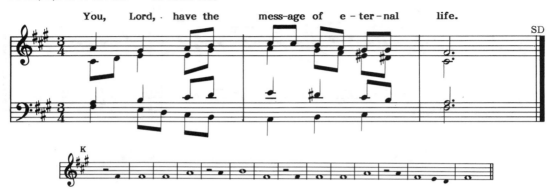

1 The láw of the Lórd is pérfect,
   it revíves the sóul.
   The rúle of the Lord is to be trústed,
   it gives wísdom to the símple.

2 The précepts of the Lórd are ríght,
   they gládden the héart.
   The commánd of the Lórd is cléar,
   it gives líght to the éyes.

3 The féar of the Lórd is hóly,
   abíding for éver.
   The decrées of the Lórd are trúth
   and áll of them júst.

4 They are móre to be desíred than góld,
   than the púrest of góld
   and swéeter are théy than hóney,
   than hóney from the cómb.

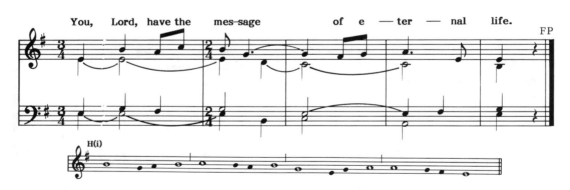

Gospel Acclamation   *John 11:25, 26*

I am the resurrection and the life, says the Lord,
whoever believes in me will never die.

  or   *John 3:16*

God loved the world so much that he gave his only Son;
everyone who believes in him has eternal life.

  When Year A readings are used   *cf. John 4:42, 15*

Lord, you are really the saviour of the world;
give me the living water, so that I may never get thirsty.

FOURTH SUNDAY OF LENT

The readings for Year A may be used as alternatives. The Psalm for Year A is 22(23), as on the Sixteenth Sunday in Ordinary Time.

Ps 136(137): 1-2. 3. 4-5. 6   R.v.6

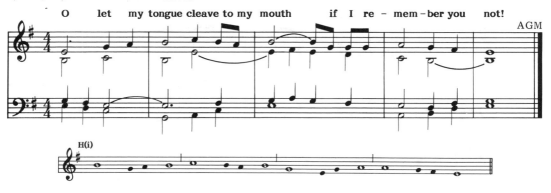

1 By the rivers of Babylon/
   there we <u>sat</u> and wept,
remem<u>be</u>ring Zion;
on the poplars <u>that</u> grew there
we <u>hung</u> up our harps.

2 For it was there that they asked us,/
   our cap<u>tors</u>, for songs,
our oppres<u>sors</u>, for joy.
'Sing to <u>us</u>,' they said,
'one of <u>Zion</u>'s songs.'

3 O how could we sing/
   the song <u>of</u> the Lord
on al<u>ien</u> soil?
If I forget you, Jerusalem
let my <u>right</u> hand wither!

4 O let my tongue/
   cleave <u>to</u> my mouth
if I remem<u>ber</u> you not,
if I prize <u>not</u> Jerusalem
above <u>all</u> my joys!

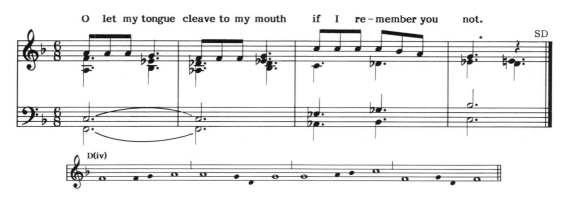

Gospel Acclamation

Luke 15:18

I will leave this place and go to my fa<u>ther</u> and say:
'Father, I have sinned against heaven and <u>against</u> you.'

When Year A readings are used

John 8:12

I am the light of the world, <u>says</u> the Lord;
anyone who follows me will have the <u>light</u> of life.

FIFTH SUNDAY OF LENT

*The readings of Year A may be used as alternatives. The Psalm for Year A is Ps
129(130), as on the Tenth Sunday in Ordinary Time.*

Ps 50(51): 3-4. 12-13. 14-15.

1 Have mércy on me, Gód, in your kíndness.
   In your compássion blot oút my offénce.
   O wásh me more and móre from my gúilt
   and cléanse me fróm my sín.

2 A púre heart creáte for me, O Gód,
   put a stéadfast spírit withín me.
   Do not cást me awáy from your présence,
   nor depríve me of your hóly spírit.

3 Give me agáin the jóy of your hélp;
   with a spírit of férvour sustáin me,
   that I may teách transgréssors your wáys
   and sínners may retúrn to yóu.

Gospel Acclamation   *John 12:26*

If a man serves me, says the Lord, he must follow me,
wherever I am, my servant will be there too.

When Year A readings are used   *John 11:25,26*
I am the resurrection and the life, says the Lord;
whoever believes in me will never die.

PASSION SUNDAY (PALM SUNDAY)

Ps 21(22): 8-9. 17-18. 19-20. 23-24.   *R.v.1*

1 All who see <u>me</u> deride me.
    They curl their lips, they <u>toss</u> their heads.
    'He trusted in the Lord, <u>let</u> him save him;
    let him release him if this <u>is</u> his friend.'

2 Many dogs <u>have</u> surrounded me,
    a band of the wick<u>ed</u> beset me.
    They tear holes in my hands <u>and</u> my feet
    I can count every one <u>of</u> my bones.

3 They divide my clothing among them.
    They cast lots <u>for</u> my robe.
    O Lord, do not leave <u>me</u> alone,
    my strength, make <u>haste</u> to help me!

4 I will tell of your name to my brethren/
        and praise you where they <u>are</u> assembled.
    'You who fear the Lord <u>give</u> him praise;
    all sons of Jacob, <u>give</u> him glory.
    Revere him, Isr<u>ael's</u> sons.'

Psalm tone as above

Gospel Acclamation   *Philippians 2:8-9*

Christ was humbler yet,/
    even to accepting death,
death <u>on</u> a cross.
* But God <u>raised</u> him high
and gave him the name/
    which is above all names.

* *repeat chant*   *or see Good Friday*   21

HOLY THURSDAY

Ps 115(116): 12-13. 15-16. 17-18.   *R.cf.1 Corinthians 10:16*

The bless-ing cup that we bless is a com-mun-ion with the blood of Christ.

1. Hów can I repáy the Lórd
   for his góod*ness* to mé?
   The cúp of salvátion *I* will ráise;
   I will cáll on *the* Lórd's náme.

2. O précious in the éyes *of* the Lórd
   is the déath *of* his fáithful.
   Your sérvant, Lord, your sér*vant* am I;
   you have lóos*ened* my bónds.

3. A thánksgiving sácri*fice* I máke:
   I will cáll on the Lór*d's* name.
   My vóws to the Lórd I *will* fulfíl
   befóre *all* his péople.

The bless-ing cup that we bless is a com-mun-ion with the blood of Christ.

Gospel Acclamation

I give you a *new* commandment:
love one another just as I have loved you, *says* the Lord.

GOOD FRIDAY

Ps 30(31): 2, 6. 12. 12-13. 15-16. 17-18.   R.v.6

1 In you, O Lord, I take refuge./
   Let me never be <u>put</u> to shame.
   In your justice, <u>set</u> me free.
   Into your hands I com<u>mend</u> my spirit.
   It is you who will re<u>deem</u> me, Lord.

2 In the face of <u>all</u> my foes
   I am <u>a</u> reproach,
   an object of scorn <u>to</u> my neighbours
   and of fear <u>to</u> my friends.

3 Those who see me <u>in</u> the street
   run <u>far</u> away from me.
   I am like a dead man, forgotten <u>in</u> men's hearts,
   like a thing <u>thrown</u> away.

4 But as for me, I trust <u>in</u> you, Lord,
   I say: 'You <u>are</u> my God.'
   My life is in your <u>hands</u>, deliver me
   from the hands of <u>those</u> who hate me.

5 Let your face shine <u>on</u> your servant.
   Save me <u>in</u> your love.
   Be strong, let your <u>heart</u> take courage,
   all who hope <u>in</u> the Lord.

Gospel Acclamation   *Philippians 2:8-9.*

Palm Sunday: use acclamation L7 (supplement). Good Friday: L4

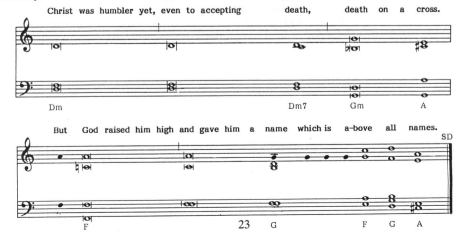

THE EASTER VIGIL

Psalm after the First Reading

Ps 103(104): 1-2. 5-6. 10. 12-14. 24, 35.   R.v.30

1   Bless thé Lord, my sóul,
    Lord Gód, hów great yóu are,
    clothed in májesty and glóry,
    wrapped in líght as ín a robe.

2   You founded thé earth on íts base,
    to stand fírm fróm age tó age.
    You wrapped it with the ócean like a clóak:
    the waters stood hígher thán the mountains.

3   You make springs gúsh forth in the valleys:
    they flów ín between the hílls.
    On their banks dwell the bírds of héaven;
    from the bránches they síng their song.

24

4 From your dwelling yóu water thé hills;
earth drínks íts fill of yóur gift.
You make the grass grów for the cáttle
and the plánts to sérve man's needs.

5 How many áre your works, Ó Lord.
In wísdom yóu have made thém all.
The earth is fúll of your ríches.
Bless the Lórd, my soul.

Send forth your Spi - rit, O Lord, and re - new the face of the earth.

AGM

E(i)

Alternative Psalm after the First Reading

Ps 32(33): 4-5. 6-7. 12-13. 20, 22   R.v.5

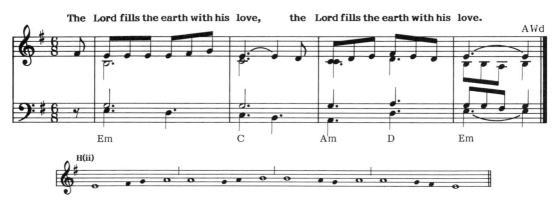

The Lord fills the earth with his love, the Lord fills the earth with his love.

AWd

Em   C   Am   D   Em

H(ii)

1 The word of the Lord is faithful
and all his works to be trusted.
The Lord loves justice and right
and fills the earth with his love.

2 By his word the heavens were made,
by the breath of his mouth all the stars.
He collects the waves of the ocean;
he stores up the depths of the sea.

3 They are happy, whose God is the Lord,
the people he has chosen as his own.
From the heavens the Lord looks forth,
he sees all the children of men.

4 Our soul is waiting for the Lord.
The Lord is our help and our shield.
May your love be upon us, O Lord,
as we place all our hope in you.

Psalm after the Second Reading

Ps 15(16): 5, 8. 9-10. 11.   R.v.1

1   O Lord, it is you who are my pórt<u>ion</u> and cup;
    it is you yourself who <u>ä</u>re my prize.
    I keep the Lord ever <u>in</u> my sight:
    since he is at my right hand, I <u>shall</u> stand firm.

2   And so my heart rejoices, my s<u>öul</u> is glad;
    even my body shall r<u>ës</u>t in safety.
    For you will not leave my soul <u>among</u> the dead,
    nor let your beloved <u>know</u> decay.

3   You will show me the p<u>äth</u> of life,
    the fullness of joy <u>in</u> your presence,   *(omit c)*
    at your right hand happ<u>iness</u> for ever.

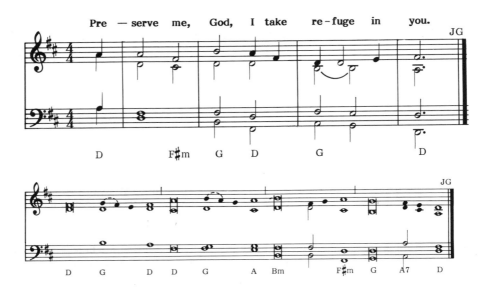

Psalm after the Third Reading

Exodus 15: 1-2. 3-5. 6. 17-18.   R.v.1

* I will síng to the Lórd: glórious his tríumph!

(repeat A)   Hórse and ríder he has thrówn <u>in</u>to the séa.
The Lórd is my stréngth, my <u>sóng</u>, my salvátion.
Thís is my Gód and <u>Í</u> éxtol him.
My fáther's Gód and I gíve him praise.

The Lórd is a wárrior, the Lórd <u>is</u> his náme.
The chários of Pháraoh he húrled <u>ín</u>to the séa,
the flówer of his ármy is dró<u>wned</u> in the séa.
The déeps híde them, they <u>sá</u>nk like a stóne.

Your ríght hand, Lórd, glórious <u>in</u> its pówer,
your ríght hand, Lórd, has sh<u>á</u>ttered the énemy. *(Omit C)*
In the gréatness of your glóry you cr<u>ú</u>shed the fóe.

You will léad them and plánt them <u>ón</u> your móuntain,
the pláce, O Lórd, where you have má<u>de</u> your hóme,
the sánctuary, Lórd, which your <u>hán</u>ds have máde,
the Lórd will reígn for <u>é</u>ver and éver.

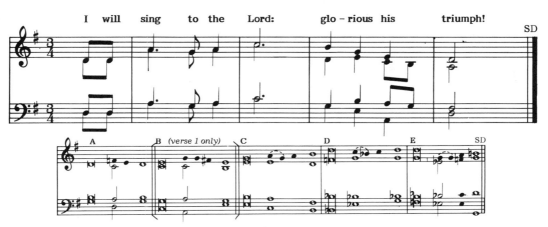

* use accents for first tone, underlinings for second

27

Psalm after the Fourth Reading

Ps 29(30): 2, 4. 5-6. 11-13   R.v.2

1   I will praise you, Lord, you have rescued me
    and have not let my enemies rejoice over me.
    O Lord, you have raised my soul from the dead,
    restored me to life from those who sink into the grave.

2   Sing psalms to the Lord, you who love him,
    give thanks to his holy name.
    His anger lasts but a moment; his favour through life.
    At night there are tears, but joy comes with dawn.

3   The Lord listened and had pity.
    The Lord came to my help.
    For me you have changed my mourning into dancing,
    O Lord my God, I thank you for ever.

Psalm tone as above.

Psalm after the Fifth Reading

Isaiah 12: 2-3. 4. 5-6.   R.v.3

1 Truly God is my salvation,/
    I trust, I shall not fear.
   For the Lord is my strength, my song,
   he became my saviour.
   With joy you will draw water/
       from the wells of salvation.

2 Give thanks to the Lord, give praise to his name! *(omit B)*
   make his mighty deeds known to the peoples,
   declare the greatness of his name.

3 Sing a psalm to the Lord/
       for he has done glorious deeds,
   make them known to all the earth!
   People of Zion, sing and shout for joy
   for great in your midst is the Holy One of Israel.

For another setting see the Baptism of the Lord, Year B, p.14

Psalm after the Sixth Reading

Ps 18(19): 8. 9. 10. 11.   R. John 6:68

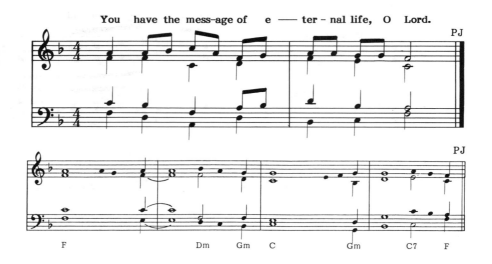

You have the mess-age of e — ter - nal life, O Lord.

F   Dm   Gm   C   Gm   C7   F

1 The law of the Lord is perfect,
   it revives the soul.
   The rule of the Lord is to be trusted,
   it gives wisdom to the simple.

2 The precepts of the Lord are right,
   they gladden the heart.
   The command of the Lord is clear,
   it gives light to the eyes.

3 The fear of the Lord is holy,
   abiding for ever.
   The decrees of the Lord are truth
   and all of them just.

4 They are more to be desired than gold,
   than the purest of gold
   and sweeter are they than honey,
   than honey from the comb.

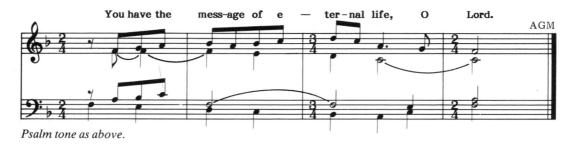

You have the mess-age of e — ter-nal life, O Lord.

Psalm tone as above.

Psalm after the Seventh Reading

Ps 41(42): 3. 5; 42(43): 3. 4   R.Ps 41(42):2

If a Baptism takes place the Responsorial Psalm which follows the Fifth Reading is used, or Ps 50(51) as on the Fifth Sunday of Lent.

1 My soul is thirsting fór God,
   the God <u>of</u> my <u>life</u>;
   when can I en<u>ter</u> ánd see
   the <u>face</u> of God?

2 These things will I remember/
      as I pour <u>out</u> mý soul:
   how I would lead the rejoicing crowd/
      into the <u>house</u> of God,
   amid cries of gladness <u>and</u> thánksgiving,
   the throng <u>wild</u> with joy.

3 O send forth your light <u>and</u> yóur truth;
   let these <u>be</u> my guide.
   Let them bring me to your <u>holý</u> mountain
   to the place <u>where</u> you dwell.

4 And I will come to the al<u>tar</u> óf God,
   the God <u>of</u> my joy.
   My redeemer, I will thank you <u>on</u> the harp,
   O <u>God</u>, my God.

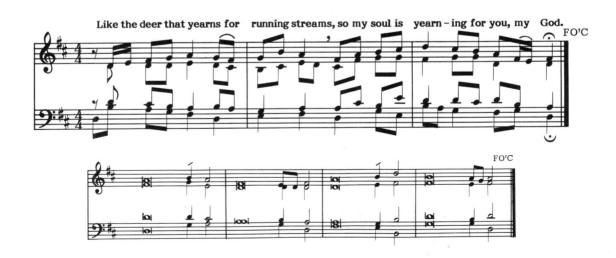

After the last Old Testament reading the priest or cantor intones the Alleluia:

The Psalm follows straight away.

Ps 117(118): 1-2. 16-17. 22-23.

1 Give thanks to the Lord for he is good,
   for his love hás no end.
   Let the sons of Israel sáy:
   'His lóve has no énd.'

2 The Lord's right hand has triumphed;
   his right hand has ráised me up.
   I shall not die, I shall líve
   and recóunt his deeds.

3 The stone which the builders rejected
   has becóme the corner stone.
   This is the work of the Lórd,
   a márvel in our eyes.

32

EASTER SUNDAY

Ps 117(118): 1-2. 16-17. 22-23.   *R.v.24*

1 Give thanks to the Lord for <u>he</u> is good,
  for his love <u>has</u> no end.
  Let the sons of Is<u>ra</u>el say:
  'His love <u>has</u> no end.'

2 The Lord's right <u>hand</u> has triumphed;
  his right hand has <u>raised</u> me up.
  I shall not die, <u>I</u> shall live
  and re<u>count</u> his deeds.

3 The stone which the buil<u>ders</u> rejected
  has become the <u>cor</u>ner stone.
  This is the work <u>of</u> the Lord,
  a marvel <u>in</u> our eyes.

Psalm tone as at the Vigil (opposite).

After the Second Reading the Sequence Victimae Paschali *is sung, followed by the Gospel Acclamation.*

Gospel Acclamation   *1 Corinthians 5:7-8*

Christ, our passover, <u>has</u> been sacrificed;
let us celebrate the feast then, <u>in</u> the Lord.

SECOND SUNDAY OF EASTER

Ps 117(118): 2-4. 13-15. 22-24. R.v.1

1 Let the sons of Israel say:/
   'His love <u>has</u> no end.'
  Let the sons of Aaron say:/
   'His love <u>has</u> no end.'
  Let those who fear <u>the</u> Lord say:
  'His love <u>has</u> no end.'

2 The stone which the builders rejected/
   has become the <u>cor</u>ner stone.
  This is the work of the Lord,/
   a marvel <u>in</u> our eyes.
  This day was made <u>by</u> the Lord;
  we rejoice <u>and</u> are <u>glad</u>.

3 O Lord, grant us salvation;/
   O Lord, <u>grant</u> success.
  Blessed in <u>the</u> name of the Lord/
   is <u>he</u> who comes.
  We bless you from the house <u>of</u> the Lord;
  the Lord God <u>is</u> our light.

Psalm tone as above.

Gospel Acclamation

John 20:29

Jesus said: 'You believe because you <u>can</u> see me.
Happy are those who have not seen and <u>yet</u> believe.'

THIRD SUNDAY OF EASTER

Ps 4: 2. 4. 7. 9.   *R.v.7*

1   When I call, answer me, O <u>God</u> of justice;
   from anguish you released me, have mer<u>cy</u> and hear me!

2   It is the Lord who grants favours to those <u>whom</u> he loves;
   the Lord hears me whene<u>ver</u> I call him.

3   'What can bring us happiness? <u>many</u> say.
   Lift up the light of your face on <u>us</u>, O Lord.

4   I will lie down in peace and sleep <u>comes</u> at once,
   for you alone, Lord, make me <u>dwell</u> in safety.

Gospel Acclamation   *Luke 24:32*

Lord Jesus, explain the scrip<u>tures</u> to us.
Make our hearts burn within us as you <u>talk</u> to us.

FOURTH SUNDAY OF EASTER

Ps 117(118): 1, 8-9. 21-23. 26, 28-9.   *R.v.22*

1   Give thanks to the Lord for he is good,/
    for his love <u>has</u> no end.
It is better to take refuge in the Lord/
    than to <u>trust</u> in men:
it is better to take refuge <u>in</u> the Lord
than to <u>trust</u> in princes.

2   I will thank you for you have given answer/
    and you <u>are</u> my saviour.
The stone which the builders rejected/
    has become the <u>corner</u> stone.
This is the work <u>of</u> the Lord,
a marvel <u>in</u> our eyes.

3   Blessed in the name of the Lord/
    is <u>he</u> who comes.
We bless you from the house <u>of</u> the Lord;
I will thank you for you have given answer/
    and you <u>are</u> my saviour.
Give thanks to the Lord for he is good;/
    for his love <u>has</u> no end.

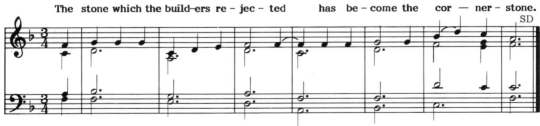

Psalm tone as above.

Gospel Acclamation   *John 10:14*

I am the good shepherd, <u>says</u> the Lord;
I know my own sheep and <u>my</u> <u>own</u> know me.

FIFTH SUNDAY OF EASTER

Ps 21(22): 26-27. 28, 30, 31-32.   R.v.26

You, Lord, are my praise in the great as — sem - bly.

1 My vows I will pay before those who fear him.
   The poor shall eat and shall have their fill.
   They shall praise the Lord, those who seek him.
   May their hearts live for ever and ever.

2 All the earth shall remember and return to the Lord,
   all families of the nations worship before him.
   They shall worship him, all the mighty of the earth;
   before him shall bow all who go down to the dust.

3 And my soul shall live for him, my children serve him.
   They shall tell of the Lord to generations yet to come,
   declare his faithfulness to peoples yet unborn:
   'These things the Lord has done.'

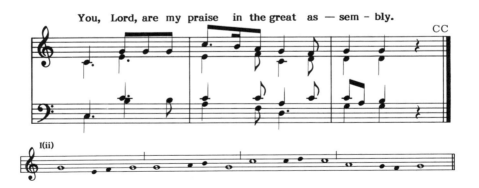

You, Lord, are my praise in the great as — sem - bly.

Gospel Acclamation   *John 15:4-5*

Make your home in me, as I make mine in you.
Whoever remains in me bears fruit in plenty.

SIXTH SUNDAY OF EASTER

Ps 97(98): 1-2. 3. 4.   *R.cf.v.2*

The Lord has shown his sal — va-tion to the na — tions.

1 Sing a new song to the Lord
for he has worked wonders.
His right hand and his holy arm
have brought salvation.

2 The Lord has made known his salvation;
has shown his justice to the nations.
He has remembered his truth and love
for the house of Israel.

3 All the ends of the earth have seen
the salvation of our God.
Shout to the Lord all the earth,
ring out your joy.

The Lord has shown his sal – va – tion to the na — tions.

Gospel Acclamation   *John 14:23*

Jesus said: 'If anyone loves me he will keep my word,
and my Father will love him, and we shall come to him.'

THE ASCENSION OF THE LORD

Ps 46(47): 2-3. 6-7. 8-9.   R.v.6

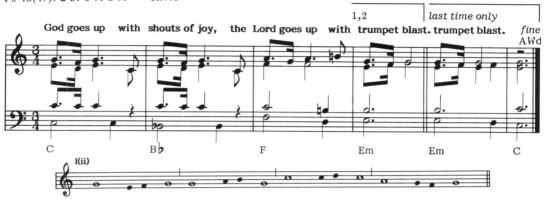

God goes up with shouts of joy, the Lord goes up with trumpet blast. trumpet blast.

1   All peoples, clap your hands,
    cry to God with shouts of joy!
    For the Lord, the Most High, we must fear,
    great king over all the earth.

2   God goes up with shouts of joy;
    the Lord goes up with trumpet blast.
    Sing praise for Gód, sing praise,
    sing praise to our king, sing praise.

3   God is the king of all the earth.
    Sing praise with all your skill.
    God is king óver the nations;
    God reigns on his holy throne.

God goes up with shouts of joy; al — le-lu — ia!

Gospel Acclamation   *Matthew 18:19-20*

Go, make disciples of all the nations;
I am with you always; yes, to the end of time.

SEVENTH SUNDAY OF EASTER

Ps 102(103): 1-2. 11-12. 19-20.   R.v.19

1 My sóul, give thánks <u>to</u> the Lórd,
   all my béing, bléss his <u>holy</u> náme.
   My sóul, give thánks <u>to</u> the Lórd
   and néver forgét <u>all</u> his bléssings.

2 For as the héavens are hígh <u>above</u> the éarth
   so stróng is his lóve for <u>those</u> who féar him.
   As fár as the éast is <u>from</u> the wést
   so fár does he re<u>móve</u> our síns.

3 The Lórd has set his swáy in héaven
   and his kíngdom is rú<u>ling</u> over áll.
   Give thánks to the Lórd, <u>all</u> his ángels,
   mighty in pówer, fulfíl<u>ling</u> his wórd.

Gospel Acclamation   *cf. John 14:18*

I will not leave you orphans, <u>says</u> the Lord;
I will come back to you, and <u>your</u> hearts will be <u>full</u> of joy.

40

PENTECOST SUNDAY
Mass during the day

Ps 103(104): 1, 24. 29-30. 31, 34.   R.v.30

1 Bless the <u>Lord</u>, my soul!
   Lord God, how <u>great</u> you are,
   How many are your <u>works</u>, O Lord!
   The earth is full <u>of</u> your riches.

3 May the glory of the Lord <u>last</u> for ever!
   May the Lord rejoice <u>in</u> his works!
   May my thoughts be <u>pleasing</u> to him.
   I find my joy <u>in</u> the Lord.

2 You take back your sp<u>irit</u>, they die,
   returning to the dust from <u>which</u> they came.
   You send forth your spirit, they <u>are</u> created;
   and you renew the face <u>of</u> the earth.

Psalm tone as above.

Other settings of this Response may be found on page 25.

After the Second Reading the sequence Veni Sancte Spiritus *is sung.*

Gospel Acclamation

Come, Holy Spirit, fill the hearts <u>of</u> the faithful,
and kindle in them the fire <u>of</u> your love.

THE MOST HOLY TRINITY

Ps 32(33):4-5. 6, 9. 18-19. 20, 22   R.v.12

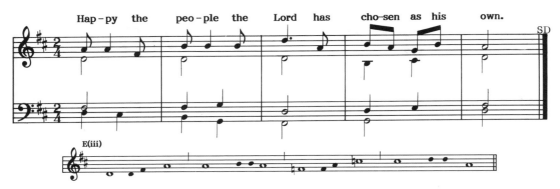

1 The word of the Lord is faithful
   and all his works to be trusted
   The Lord loves justice and right
   and fills the earth with his love.

2 By his word the heavens were made,
   by the breath of his mouth all the stars.
   He spoke; and they came to be.
   He commanded; they sprang into being.

3 The Lord looks on those who revere him,
   on those who hope in his love,
   to rescue their souls from death,
   to keep them alive in famine.

4 Our soul is waiting for the Lord.
   The Lord is our help and our shield.
   May your love be upon us, O Lord,
   as we place all our hope in you.

Gospel Acclamation

cf. Apocalypse 1:8

Glory be to the Father, and to the Son, and to the Holy Spirit,
the God who is, who was, and who is to come.

42

THE BODY AND BLOOD OF CHRIST
(Corpus Christi)

Ps 115(116):12-13. 15-16. 17-18.   *R.v.13*

1   How can I repay the Lord
for his goodness to me?
The cup of salvation I will raise;
I will call on the Lord's name.

2   O precious in the eyes of the Lord
is the death of his faithful.
Your servant, Lord, your servant am I;
you have loosened my bonds.

3   A thanksgiving sacrifice I make:
I will call on the Lord's name.
My vows to the Lord I will fulfil
before all his people.

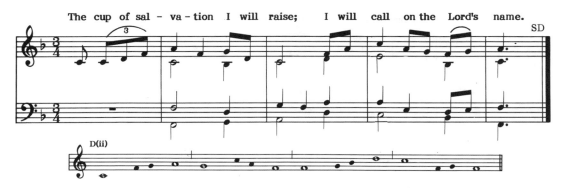

The sequence Lauda Sion *may be sung in whole or in part.*

Gospel Acclamation   *John 6:51-52*

I am the living bread which has come down from heaven, says the Lord.
Anyone who eats this bread will live for ever.

SECOND SUNDAY IN ORDINARY TIME

Ps 39(40): 2, 4. 7-8. 9. 10   R.vv.8-9

JR

1 I waited, I waited <u>for</u> the Lord
   and he stooped <u>down</u> to me;
   He put a new song in<u>to</u> my mouth,
   praise <u>of</u> our God.

2 You do not ask for sacri<u>fice</u> and offerings,
   but an <u>open</u> ear.
   You do <u>not</u> ask for holo<u>caust</u> and victim.
   Instead, <u>here</u> am I.

3 In the scroll of the book <u>it</u> stands written
   that I should <u>do</u> your will.
   My God, I delight <u>in</u> your law
   in the depth <u>of</u> my heart.

4 Your justice I <u>have</u> proclaimed
   in the <u>great</u> assembly.
   My lips <u>I have</u> not sealed;
   you know <u>it</u>, O Lord.

SD

Gospel Acclamation

1 Samuel 3:9

Speak, Lord, your serv<u>ant</u> is listening:
you have the message of et<u>ernal</u> life.

or   *John 1:41.17*

We have found the Messiah – which <u>means</u> the Christ –
grace and truth have <u>come</u> through him.

THIRD SUNDAY IN ORDINARY TIME

Ps 24(25):4-5. 6-7. 8-9.   R.v.4

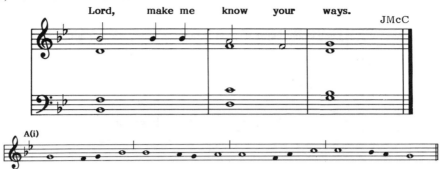

1 Lord, make me <u>know</u> your ways.
   Lord, teach <u>me</u> your paths.
   Make me walk in your <u>truth</u>, and teach me:
   for you are <u>God</u> my saviour.

2 Remember your <u>mer</u>cy, Lord,
   and the love you have shown <u>from</u> of old.
   In your love re<u>mem</u>ber me,
   because of your good<u>ness</u>, O Lord.

3 The Lord is <u>good</u> and upright.
   He shows the <u>path</u> to <u>those</u> who stray,
   He guides the humble in <u>the</u> right path;
   he teaches his way <u>to</u> the poor.

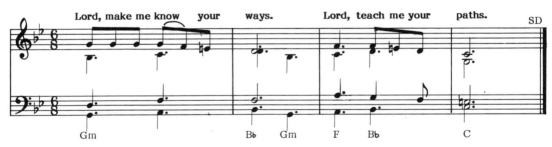

Psalm tone as above

Gospel Acclamation   *Mark 1:15*

The kingdom of God is <u>close</u> at hand;
believe <u>the</u> Good News.

FOURTH SUNDAY IN ORDINARY TIME

Ps 94(95): 1-2. 6-7. 8-9   R.v.9

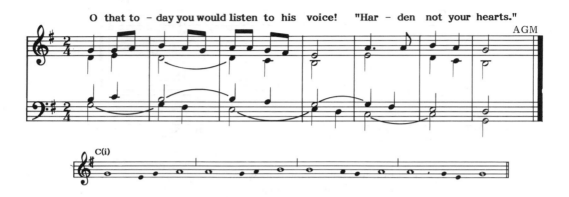

1 Come, ring out our joy to the Lord;
   hail the rock who saves us.
   Let us come before him, giving thanks,
   with songs let us hail the Lord.

2 Come in; let us kneel and bend low;
   let us kneel before God who made us
   for he is our God/and we
   the people who belong to his pasture,
   the flock that is led by his hand.

3 O that today you would listen to his voice!/
     'Harden not your hearts as at Meribah,
   as on that day at Massah in the desert
   when your fathers put me to the test;
   when they tried me, though they saw my work.'

Gospel Acclamation   *Matthew 11:25*

Blessed are you, Father,/
  Lord of heaven and earth,
for revealing the mysteries of the kingdom/
  to mere children.

or   *Matthew 4:16*

The people that lived in darkness/
  has seen a great light;
on those who dwell in the land and shadow of death/
  a light has dawned.

FIFTH SUNDAY IN ORDINARY TIME

Ps 146(147):1. 2-4. 5-6.   *R.v.3*

1 Praise the Lord for <u>he</u> is good;
  sing to our God for <u>he</u> is loving: *(omit c)*
to him our <u>praise</u> is due.

2 The Lord builds up Jerusalem/
  and brings back Is<u>ra</u>el's exiles,
   he heals the broken-hearted,/
he binds up <u>all</u> their wounds.
He fixes the number <u>of</u> the stars;
he calls each one <u>by</u> its name.

3 Our Lord is great <u>and</u> almighty;
his wisdom can ne<u>ver</u> be measured.
The Lord ra<u>ises</u> the lowly;
he humbles the wicked <u>to</u> the dust.

optional ending:

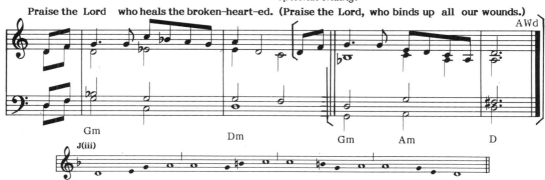

Gospel Acclamation   *John 8:12*   *Matthew 8:17*

I am the light of the world, <u>says</u> the Lord,   *or*
anyone who follows me/
  will have the <u>light</u> of life.   He took our sicknes<u>ses</u> away,
                                    and carried our dis<u>ea</u>ses for us.

SIXTH SUNDAY IN ORDINARY TIME

Ps 31(32): 1-2. 5-6. 11   R.v.7

alternative psalm tone: from group E

1 Happy the mán whose offénce <u>is</u> forgíven,
   whose sín <u>is</u> remítted.
   O háppy the mán to whom the Lórd im<u>putes</u> no gúilt,
   in whose spírit <u>is</u> no gúile.

2 But nów I have ac<u>knów</u>ledged my síns;
   my gúilt I <u>did</u> not híde.
   I sáid: 'I will conféss my offénce <u>to</u> the Lórd.'
   And yóu, Lord, have forgiven the guilt <u>óf</u> my sin.

3 Rejóice, rejóice <u>in</u> the Lórd,
   ex<u>últ</u> you júst!
   O cóme, ring <u>out</u> your jóy,
   all you <u>úpright</u> of héart.

Gospel Acclamation   *cf. Ephesians 1:17.18*

May the Father of our Lord Jesus Christ/
   enlighten the eyes <u>of</u> our mind,
so that we can see what hope his call <u>holds</u> for us.

or   *Luke 7:16*

A great prophet has app<u>ea</u>red among us;
God has visit<u>ed</u> his people.

SEVENTH SUNDAY IN ORDINARY TIME

Ps 40(41): 2-3. 4-5. 13-14.   *R.v.5*

Heal my soul, for I have sinned a-gainst you.

1 Happy the man who considers the poor <u>and</u> the weak.
   The Lord will save him in the <u>day</u> of evil,
   will guard him, give him life, <u>make</u> him happy <u>in</u> the land
   and will not give him up to the will <u>of</u> his foes.

2 The Lord will help him on his <u>bed</u> of pain,
   he will bring him back from sick<u>ness</u> to health.
   As for me, I said: 'Lord, have <u>mer</u>cy on me,
   heal my soul for I have <u>sinned</u> against you.'

3 If you uphold me I shall <u>be</u> unharmed
   and set in your presence for <u>ev</u>ermore.
   Blessed be the Lord, the <u>God</u> of Israel
   from age to age. A<u>men</u>. Amen.

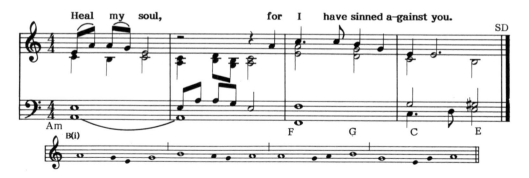

Heal my soul, for I have sinned a-gainst you.

Gospel Acclamation   *John 1:14.12*

The Word was made flesh and <u>lived</u> among us;
to all who did accept him/
   he gave power to become child<u>ren</u> of God.

or   *Luke 4:18*

The Lord has sent me to bring the good news <u>to</u> the poor,
to proclaim liberty to cap<u>tives</u>.

EIGHTH SUNDAY IN ORDINARY TIME

Ps 102(103): 1-2. 3-4. 8, 10. 12-13   R.v.8

1 My sóul, give thánks <u>to</u> the Lórd,
   all my béing, bléss his <u>ho</u>ly náme.
   My sóul, give thánks <u>to</u> the Lórd
   and néver forgét <u>all</u> his bléssings.

2 It is hé who forgíves <u>all</u> your gúilt,
   who héals every óne <u>of</u> your ílls,
   who redeéms your lífe <u>from</u> the gráve,
   who cró wns you with lóve <u>and</u> compássion.

3 The Lórd is compás<u>sion</u> and lóve,
   slow to ánger and <u>rích</u> in mércy.
   He does not tréat us accórding <u>to</u> our síns,
   nor repáy us accórding <u>to</u> our faùlts.

4 As fár as the eást is <u>from</u> the wést
   so fár does he re<u>móve</u> our síns.
   As a fáther has compássion <u>on</u> his sóns,
   the Lord has píty on <u>thó</u>se who féar him.

Gospel Acclamation   *John 10:27*

The sheep that belong to me listen to my voice,/
  <u>says</u> the Lord.
I know them <u>and</u> they follow me.

or   *James 1:18*

By his own choice the Father made us his children/
  by the message <u>of</u> the truth,
so that we should <u>be</u> a sort of first-fruits/
  of all that <u>he</u> created.

NINTH SUNDAY IN ORDINARY TIME

Ps 80(81): 3-4. 5-6. 7-8. 10-11.   R.v.2

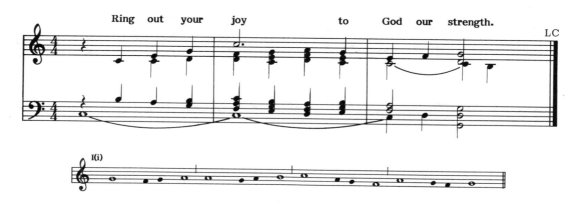

1 Raise a song and <u>sound</u> the timbrel,
the sweet-sounding harp <u>and</u> the lute,
blow the trumpet <u>at</u> the new moon,
when the moon is full, <u>on</u> our feast.

2 For this is Is<u>ra</u>el's law,
a command of the <u>God</u> of Jacob.
He imposed it as a <u>rule</u> on Joseph,
when he went out against the <u>land</u> of Egypt.

3 A voice I did not know <u>said</u> to me:
'I freed your shoulder <u>from</u> the burden;
your hands were freed <u>from</u> the load.
You called in distress <u>and</u> I saved you.

4 'Let there be no foreign <u>god</u> among you,
no worship of an a<u>lien god</u>.
I am the <u>Lord</u> your God,
who brought you from the <u>land</u> of Egypt.'

Gospel Acclamation

cf. John 6:63.68

Your words are spirit, Lord,/
   and <u>they</u> are life:
you have the message of et<u>er</u>nal life.

or

cf. John 17:17

Your word is tr<u>uth</u>, O Lord,
consecrate us in the tr<u>uth</u>.

TENTH SUNDAY IN ORDINARY TIME

Ps 129(130): 1-2. 3-4. 5-6. 7-8.   *R.v.7*

With the Lord there is mer-cy and full-ness of re-demp-tion.

AGM

1 Out of the depths I cry to <u>you</u>, O Lord,
   Lord, <u>hear</u> my voice!
   O let your ears <u>be</u> attentive
   to the voice <u>of</u> my pleading.

2 If you, O Lord, should <u>mark</u> our guilt
   Lord, who <u>would</u> survive?
   But with you is <u>found</u> forgiveness:
   for this <u>we</u> revere you.

3 My soul is waiting <u>for</u> the Lord,
   I count <u>on</u> his word.
   My soul is longing <u>for</u> the Lord
   More than watchman <u>for</u> daybreak.

4 Because with the Lord <u>there</u> is mercy
   and fullness <u>of</u> redemption,
   Israel indeed he <u>will</u> redeem
   from all <u>its</u> iniquity.

Gospel Acclamation

John 14:23

If anyone loves me he will <u>keep</u> my word,
and my Father will love him, and <u>we</u> shall come to him.

or

John 12:31-32

Now the prince of this world is to be overthrown,/
   <u>says</u> the Lord.
And when I am lifted up from the earth/
   I shall draw all men <u>to</u> myself.

ELEVENTH SUNDAY IN ORDINARY TIME

Ps 91(92): 2-3. 13. 14-16.   *R.cf.v.2*

It is good to give you thanks, O Lord.

JMcC

1 It is good to give thanks <u>to</u> the Lord
to make music to your name, <u>O</u> Most High
to proclaim your love <u>in</u> the morning
and your truth in the watches <u>of</u> the night.

2 The just will flourish <u>like</u> the palm-tree   *(Omit B and C)*
and grow like a Le<u>ba</u>non cedar.

3 Planted in the house of the Lord/
they will flourish in the courts <u>of</u> our God,
still bearing fruit when they are old,/
still full of <u>sap</u>, still green,
to proclaim that the <u>Lord</u> is just.
In him, my rock, there <u>is</u> no wrong.

Gospel Acclamation   *John 15:15*

I call you friends, says the Lord,/
because I have made k<u>no</u>wn to you
everything I have learnt <u>from</u> my Father.

or

The seed is the word of God, Christ the sower;
whoever finds this seed will rem<u>ain</u> for ever.

TWELFTH SUNDAY IN ORDINARY TIME

Ps 106(107): 23-24. 25-26. 28-29. 30-31.   R.v.1

O give thanks to the Lord, for his love en-dures for e — ver.

1 Some sailed to the sea in ships
   to trade on the mighty waters.
   These men have séen the Lord's deeds,
   the wonders he does in the deep.

2 For he spoke; he summoned the gale.
   tossing the waves of the sea.
   up to the heaven and back ínto the deep;
   their soul melted away in their distress.

3 Then they cried to the Lord in their need
   and he rescued them from their distress.
   He stilled the stórm to a whisper:
   all the waves of the sea were hushed.

4 They rejoiced because of the calm
   and he led them to the haven they desired.
   Let them thank the Lórd for his love,
   the wonders he does for men.

O give thanks to the Lord, for his love en-dures for ev — er.

Gospel Acclamation

cf. Ephesians 1:17.18

May the Father of our Lord Jesus Christ/
   enlighten the eyes of our mind,
so that we can see what hope his call holds for us.

or

Luke 7:16

A great prophet has appeared among us;
God has visited his people.

THIRTEENTH SUNDAY IN ORDINARY TIME

The Psalm for today is the same as that for the Fourth Reading of the Easter Vigil on page 28.

Gospel Acclamation

cf. John 6:63.68   or   cf. 2 Timothy 1:10

Your words are spirit, Lord, and they are life:
You have the message of eternal life.

Our Saviour Christ Jesus abolished death,
and he has proclaimed life through the Good News.

FOURTEENTH SUNDAY IN ORDINARY TIME

Ps 122(123): 1-2b. 2c-3. 4-5.   R.v.3

Our eyes are on the Lord till he show us his mer-cy.

1 To yóu have I lífted up my éyes,
   you who dwéll in the héavens:
   my éyes, like the éyes of sláves
   on the hánd of their lórds.

2 Líke the éyes of a sérvant
   on the hánd of her místress,
   so our éyes are on the Lórd our Gód
   till he shów us his mércy.

3 Have mércy on us, Lórd, have mércy.
   We are fílled with cóntempt.
   Indeéd all too full is our soul/
      with the scórn of the rích,
   with the próud man's disdáin.

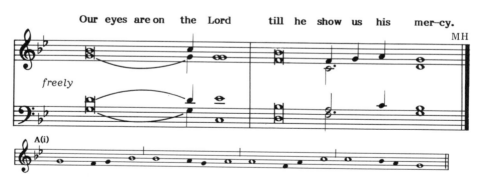

Our eyes are on the Lord till he show us his mer-cy.

freely

Gospel Acclamation   John 1:14.12

The Word was made flesh and lived among us;
to all who did accept him/
   he gave power to become children of God.

or   Luke 4:18

The spirit of the Lord has been given to me;
he has sent me to bring the Good News to the poor.

FIFTEENTH SUNDAY IN ORDINARY TIME

Ps 84(85): 9-10. 11-12. 13-14   *R.v.8*

Let us see, O Lord, your mer-cy, and give us your sa-ving help.

1 I will hear what the Lord God <u>has</u> to say,
   a voice that speaks of peace./
        peace <u>for</u> his people.
   His help is near for <u>those</u> who fear him
   and his glory will dwell <u>in</u> our land.

2 Mercy and faithful<u>ness</u> have met;
   justice and peace <u>have</u> embraced.
   Faithfulness shall spring <u>from</u> the earth
   and justice look <u>down</u> from heaven.

3 The Lord will <u>make</u> us prosper
   and our earth shall <u>yield</u> its fruit.
   Justice shall <u>march</u> before him
   and peace shall fol<u>low</u> his steps.

Alternative settings may be found on page 5.

Gospel Acclamation

cf. John 6:63.68

Your words are spirit, Lord, and <u>they</u> are life:
you have the message of e<u>ter</u>nal life.

or

cf. Ephesians 1:17.18

May the Father of our Lord Jesus Christ/
   enlighten the eyes <u>of</u> our mind,
so that we can see what hope his call <u>holds</u> for us.

SIXTEENTH SUNDAY IN ORDINARY TIME

Ps 22(23):1-3a. 3b-4. 5. 6.   R.v.1

1 The Lord is my shepherd;/
   there is nothing I shall want.
  Fresh and green are the pastures/
   where he gives me repose.
  Near restful waters he leads me,
  to revive my drooping spirit.

2 He guides me along the right path;/
   he is true to his name.
  If I should walk in the valley of darkness/
   no evil would I fear.
  You are there with your crook and your staff;
  with these you give me comfort.

3 You have prepared a banquet for me
   in the sight of my foes.
  My head you have anointed with oil;
  my cup is overflowing.

4 Surely goodness and kindness shall follow me
   all the days of my life.
  In the Lord's own house shall I dwell
  for ever and ever.

Gospel Acclamation

John 10:27

The sheep that belong to me listen to my voice, says the Lord.
I know them and they follow me.

SEVENTEENTH·SUNDAY IN ORDINARY TIME

Ps 144(145):10-11. 15-16. 17-18.   R.v.16

℟ You open wide your hand, O Lord, and grant our desires.

1 All your creatures shall thank you, O Lord,
    and your friends shall repeat their blessing.
    They shall speak of the glory of your reign
    and declare your might, O God.

2 The eyes of all creatures look to you
    and you give them their food in due time.
    You open wide your hand,
    grant the desires of all who live.

3 The Lord is just in all his ways
    and loving in all his deeds.
    He is close to all who call him,
    who call on him from their hearts.

Gospel Acclamation   *cf. John 6:63.68*

Your words are spirit, Lord, and they are life:
you have the message of eternal life.

or   *Luke 7:16*

A great prophet has appeared among us;
God has visited his people.

EIGHTEENTH SUNDAY IN ORDINARY TIME

Ps 77(78): 3-4. 23-24. 25-26.   R.v.24

1 The things we have heard and understood,
   the things our fathers have told us,
   we will tell to the next generation:
   the glories of the Lord and his might.

2 He commanded the clouds above
   and opened the gates of heaven.
   He rained down manna for their food,
   and gave them bread from heaven.

3 Mere men ate the bread of angels.
   He sent them abundance of food.
   He brought them to his holy land,
   to the mountain which his right hand had won.

Gospel Acclamation

John 14:6

I am the Way, the Truth and the Life, says the Lord;
no one can come to the Father except through me.

or

Matthew 4:4

Man does not live on bread alone,
but on every word that comes from the mouth of God.

NINETEENTH SUNDAY IN ORDINARY TIME

Ps 33(34): 2-3. 4-5. 6-7. 8-9.   R.v.9

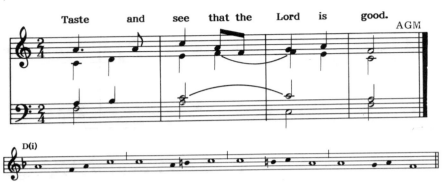

1   I will bless the Lord <u>at</u> all times,
    his praise always <u>on</u> my lips;
    in the Lord my soul shall m<u>a</u>ke its boast.
    The humble shall hear <u>and</u> be glad.

2   Glorify the L<u>or</u>d with me.
    Together let us pr<u>ai</u>se his name.
    I sought the Lord <u>and</u> he answered me;
    from all my terrors he s<u>et</u> me free.

3   Look towards him <u>and</u> be radiant;
    let your faces not <u>be</u> abashed.
    This poor man called; <u>the</u> Lord heard him
    and rescued him from all <u>his</u> distress.

4   The angel of the Lord <u>is</u> encamped
    around those who revere <u>him</u>, to rescue them.
    Taste and see that the L<u>or</u>d is good.
    He is happy who seeks ref<u>u</u>ge in him.

Gospel Acclamation   *John 14:23*

If anyone loves me he will k<u>ee</u>p my word,
and my Father will love him, and <u>we</u> shall come to him.

or   *John 6:51*

I am the living bread which has come down from heaven,
    s<u>ays</u> thé Lord.
Anyone who eats this bread will l<u>ive</u> for ever.

TWENTIETH SUNDAY IN ORDINARY TIME

The same response is used as on the 19th Sunday

Ps 33(34): 2-3. 10-11. 12-13. 14-15.   R.v.1

1 I will bless the Lord <u>at</u> all times,
   his praise always <u>on</u> my lips;
   in the Lord my soul shall m<u>a</u>ke its boast.
   The humble shall hear <u>and</u> be glad.

2 Revere the Lord, y<u>ou</u> his saints.
   They lack nothing, those w<u>ho</u> revere him.
   Strong lions suffer want <u>and</u> go hungry
   but those who seek the Lord l<u>ack</u> no blessing.

3 Come child<u>ren</u>, and hear me
   that I may teach you the fear <u>of</u> the Lord.
   Who is he who l<u>ongs</u> for life
   and many days, to enjoy <u>his</u> prosperity?

4 Then keep your t<u>ongue</u> from evil
   and your lips from speak<u>ing</u> deceit.
   Turn aside from evil <u>and</u> do good;
   seek and strive <u>after</u> peace.

Gospel Acclamation   *John 1:14.12*

The Word was made flesh and l<u>ived</u> among us;
to all who did accept him/
   he gave power to become child<u>ren</u> of God.

or   *John 6:56*

He who eats my flesh and d<u>rinks</u> my blood
lives in me and I live in him, s<u>ays</u> the Lord.

TWENTY-FIRST SUNDAY IN ORDINARY TIME

Ps 33(34): 1-2. 16-17. 18-19. 20-21. 22-23.   R.v.1

1 I will bless the Lord <u>at</u> all times,
   his praise always <u>on</u> my lips;
   in the Lord my soul shall m<u>a</u>ke its boast.
   The humble shall hear <u>and</u> be glad.

2 The Lord turns his face ag<u>ai</u>nst the wicked
   to destroy their remembrance f<u>rom</u> the earth.
   The Lord turns his eyes <u>to</u> the just
   and his ears to th<u>eir</u> appeal.

3 They call <u>and</u> the Lord hears
   and rescues them in all th<u>eir</u> distress.
   The Lord is close to the b<u>roken</u>-hearted;
   those whose spirit is crushed <u>he</u> will save.

4 Many are the trials <u>of</u> the just man
   but from them all the L<u>ord</u> will rescue him.
   He will keep guard over <u>all</u> his bones,
   not one of his bones sh<u>all</u> be broken.

5 Evil brings death to the wicked;
   those who hate the g<u>ood</u> are doomed.
   The Lord ransoms the souls <u>of</u> his servants.
   Those who hide in him shall not <u>be</u> condemned.

Gospel Acclamation   *cf. John 6:63.68*

Your words are spirit, Lord, and <u>they</u> are life:
you have the message of et<u>ernal</u> life.

TWENTY-SECOND SUNDAY
IN ORDINARY TIME

Ps 14(15): 1-2. 3-4b. 4c-5.

The just will live in the pre-sence of the Lord.

1 Lord, who shall dwéll on your hóly móuntain?
   Hé who wálks without fáult;
   hé who ácts with jústice
   and spéaks the trúth from his héart.

2 Hé who does no wróng to his bróther,
   who cásts no slúr on his néighbour,
   who hólds the gódless in disdáin,
   but hónours thóse who fear the Lórd.

3 Hé who keeps his plédge, come what máy;
   who tákes no ínterest on a lóan
   and accépts no bríbes against the ínnocent.
   Such a mán will stand fírm for éver.

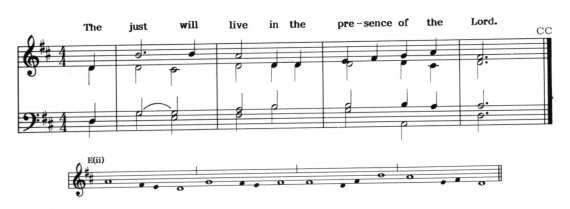

The just will live in the pre-sence of the Lord.

Gospel Acclamation   *cf. John 6:63.68*   *or*   *James 1:18*

Your words are spirit, Lord, and they are life:
you have the message of eternal life.

By his own choice the Father made us his children/
  by the message of the truth,
so that we should be a sort of first-fruits/
  of all that he created.

TWENTY-THIRD SUNDAY IN ORDINARY TIME

Ps 145(146): 6c-7. 8-9a. 9b-10.   R.v.1

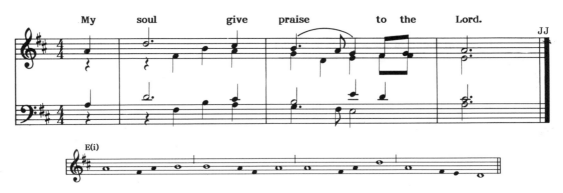

My soul give praise to the Lord.

1   It is the Lórd who keeps fáith for éver,
    who is júst to thóse who are oppréssed.
    It is hé who gives bréad to the húngry,
    the Lórd, who sets prísoners frée.

2   It is the Lórd who gives síght to the blínd,
    who raíses up thóse who are bowed dówn,
    the Lórd who lóves the júst,
    the Lórd, who protécts the stránger.

3   The Lórd upholds the wídow and órphan,
    but thwárts the páth of the wícked.
    The Lórd will reígn for éver,
    Zion's Gód, from áge to áge.

My soul, give praise to the Lord, my soul, give praise to the Lord.

Gospel Acclamation
1 Samuel 3:9, John 6:68

Speak, Lord, your servant is listening:
you have the message of eternal life.

or
cf. Matthew 4:23

Jesus proclaimed the Good News of the kingdom,
and cured all kinds of sickness among the people.

TWENTY-FOURTH SUNDAY
IN ORDINARY TIME

Ps 114(115): 1-2. 3-4. 5-6. 8-9.   *R.v.9*

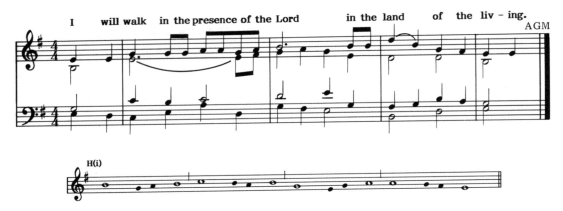

I will walk in the presence of the Lord in the land of the liv - ing.

AGM

1 I love the Lord for he has heard
   the cry of my appeal;
   for he turned his ear to me
   in the day when I called him.

2 They surround me, the snares of death,/
      with the anguish of the tomb;
   they caught me, sorrow and distress.
   I called on the Lord's name.
   O Lord my God, deliver me!

3 How gracious is the Lord, and just;
   our God has compassion.
   The Lord protects the simple hearts;
   I was helpless so he saved me.

4 He has kept my soul from death,
   my eyes from tears/
      and my feet from stumbling.
   I will walk in the presence of the Lord
   in the land of the living.

Alternative settings may be found on page 17.

Gospel Acclamation

John 14:6

I am the Way, the Truth and the Life, says the Lord;
no one can come to the Father except through me.

or

Galatians 6:14

The only thing I can boast about is the cross of our Lord Jesus Christ,
through whom the world is crucified to me, and I to the world.

TWENTY-FIFTH SUNDAY IN ORDINARY TIME

Ps 53(54): 3-4. 5. 6, 8   R.v.6

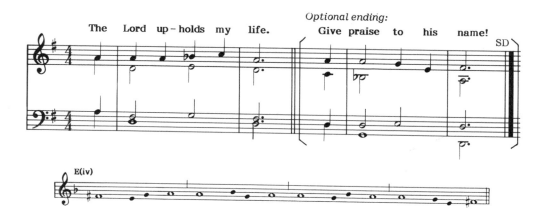

1   O God, save me by your name;
    by your power, uphold my cause.
    O God, hear my prayer;
    listen to the words of my mouth.

2   For proud men have risen against me,
    ruthless men seek my life.   *(omit C)*
    They have no regard for God.

3   But I have God for my help.
    The Lord upholds my life.
    I will sacrifice to you with willing heart
    and praise your name for it is good.

Gospel Acclamation   *John 8:12*

I am the light of the world, says the Lord,
anyone who follows me will have the light of life.

or

                                          cf. 2 Thessalonians 2:14

Through the Good News God called us
to share the glory of our Lord Jesus Christ.

TWENTY-SIXTH SUNDAY IN ORDINARY TIME

Ps 18(19): 8. 10. 12-13. 14   *R.v.9*

1　The láw of the Lórd is pérfect,
　　it revíves the sóul.
　　The rúle of the Lórd is to be trústed,
　　it gives wísdom to the símple.

2　The féar of the Lórd is hóly,
　　abíding for éver.
　　The decrées of the Lórd are trúth
　　and áll of them júst.

3　So in thém your sérvant finds instrúction;
　　great rewárd is in their kéeping.
　　But whó can detéct all his érrors?
　　From hídden faults acquít me.

4　From presúmption restráin your sérvant
　　and lét it not rúle me.
　　Thén shall I be blámeless,
　　cléan from grave sín.

Gospel Acclamation

cf. John 17:17

Your word is truth, O Lord,
consecrate us in the truth.

TWENTY-SEVENTH SUNDAY
IN ORDINARY TIME

Ps 127(128): 1-2. 3. 4-6.   R.v.5

CC

C(i)

1   O blessed are thóse who féar the Lórd
    and wálk in his wáys!
    By the lábour of your hánds you shall éat.
    You will be háppy and prósper.

2   Your wífe like a frúitful víne
    in the héart of your hóuse;
    your chíldren like shóots of the ólive,
    aróund your táble.

3   Indéed thús shall be bléssed/
        the man who féars the Lórd.
    May the Lórd bléss you from Zíon
    in a happy Jerusalem all the dáys of your lífe!
    Máy you see your chíldren's chíldren.*
    On Isr**a**el, péace!

*   * In psalm tone I(iv), repeat the last two lines.*

MH

I(iv)

Gospel Acclamation   *cf. John 17:17*

or

1 John 4:12

Your word is truth, O Lord,
consecrate us in the truth.

As long as we love one another
God will live in us/
    and his love will be complete in us.

TWENTY-EIGHTH SUNDAY
IN ORDINARY TIME

Ps 89(90): 12-13. 14-15. 16-17   R.v.14

1   Make us know the shortness of our life
     that we may gain wisdom of heart.
     Lord, relent! Is your anger for ever?
     Show pity to your servants.

2   In the morning, fill us with your love;
     we shall exult and rejoice all our days.
     Give us joy to balance our affliction
     for the years when we knew misfortune.

3   Show forth your work to your servants;
     let your glory shine on their children.
     Let the favour of the Lord be upon us:
     give success to the work of our hands.

Gospel Acclamation   *cf. Matthew 11:25*

Matthew 5:3

Blessed are you, Father,/
  Lord of heaven and earth,
for revealing the mysteries of the kingdom/
  to mere children.

or

How happy are the poor in spirit;
theirs is the kingdom of heaven.

TWENTY-NINTH SUNDAY IN ORDINARY TIME

Ps. 32(33): 4-5. 18-19. 20, 22.   *R.v.22*

1 The wórd of the Lórd is fáithful
   and áll his wórks to be trústed.
   The Lórd loves jústice and ríght
   and fills the éarth with his lóve.

2 The Lórd looks on thóse who revére him,
   on thóse who hópe in his lóve,
   to réscue their sóuls from déath,
   to keep them alíve in fámine.

3 Our sóul is wáiting for the Lórd.
   The Lórd is our hélp and our shíeld.
   May your lóve be upón us, O Lórd,
   as we pláce all our hópe in yóu.

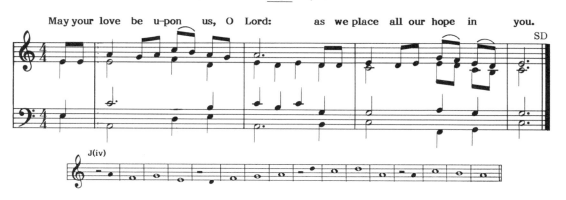

Gospel Acclamation   *John 14:6*

I am the Way, the Truth and the Life, says the Lord;
no one can come to the Father except through me.

or   *Mark 10:45*

The Son of Man came to serve,
and to give his life as a ransom for many.

THIRTIETH SUNDAY IN ORDINARY TIME

Ps 125(126): 1-2b. 3. 4-5. 6.   R.v.3

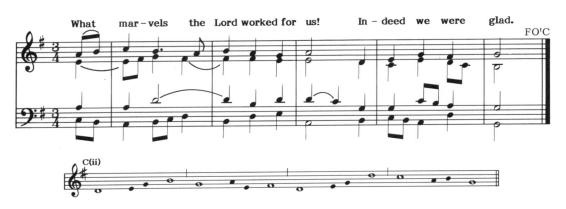

1 When the Lórd delivered Zíon from bóndage,
   It séemed like a dréam.
   Thén was our móuth filled with laúghter,
   on our líps there were sóngs.

2 The héathens themsélves said: What márvels
   the Lórd worked for thém!
   What márvels the Lórd worked for ús!
   Indéed we were glád.

3 Delíver us, O Lórd, from our bóndage
   as stréams in dry lánd.
   Thóse who are sówing in téars
   will síng when they réap.

4 They go óut, they go óut, full of téars,
   cárrying séed for the sówing:
   they come báck, they come báck, full of sóng,
   cárrying their shéaves.

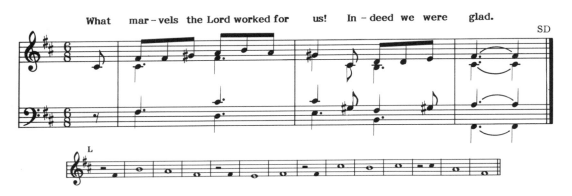

Gospel Acclamation

John 8:12

I am the light of the world, says the Lord,
anyone who follows me will have the light of life.

or

cf. 2 Timothy 1:10

Our Saviour Christ Jesus abolished death,
and he has proclaimed life through the Good News.

THIRTY-FIRST SUNDAY IN ORDINARY TIME

Ps 17(18): 2-4. 47-48.   R.v.2

1 I love you, Lord, my strength,/
      my rock, my fortress, my saviour.
   My God is the rock where I take refuge;/
      my shield, my mighty help, my stronghold.
   The Lord is worthy of all praise:
   when I call I am saved from my foes.

2 Long life to the Lord, my rock!
   Praised be the God who saves me.
   He has given great victories to his king
   and shown his love for his anointed.

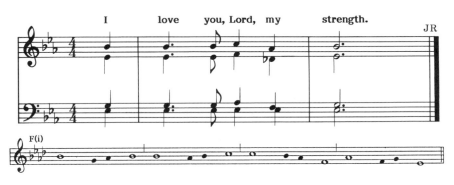

Gospel Acclamation   *cf. John 6:63.68*

or

John 14:23

Your words are spirit, Lord, and they are life:
you have the message of eternal life.

If anyone loves me he will keep my word,
and my Father will love him, and we shall come to him.

THIRTY-SECOND SUNDAY
IN ORDINARY TIME

The Psalm for today is the same as that for the 23rd Sunday, on page 63.

Gospel Acclamation

Apocalypse 2:10

Even if you have to die, says the Lord,
keep faithful, and I will give you the crown of life.

or

Matthew 5:3

How happy are the poor in spirit;
theirs is the kingdom of heaven.

THIRTY-THIRD SUNDAY IN ORDINARY TIME

The Psalm for today is the same as that for the Second Reading of the Easter Vigil on page 26.

Gospel Acclamation   *Matthew 24:42.44*   *Luke 21:36*

Stay awake and stand ready,
because you do not know the hour/
when the Son of Man is coming.

or

Stay awake, praying at all times
for the strength to stand with confidence/
before the Son of Man.

Last Sunday in Ordinary Time
OUR LORD JESUS CHRIST, UNIVERSAL KING

Ps 92(93): 1abc. 1d-2. 5.   *R.v.1*

1 The Lord is king, with majesty enrobed;
   the Lord has robed himself with might,
   he has girded himself with power.

2 The World you made firm, not to be moved;
   your throne has stood firm from of old.
   From all eternity, O Lord, you are.

3 Truly your decrees are to be trusted.
   Holiness is fitting to your house,
   O Lord, until the end of time.

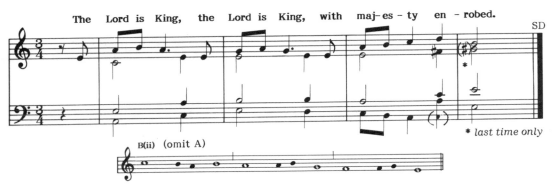

Gospel Acclamation   *Mark 11:9.10*

Blessings on him who comes in the name of the Lord!
Blessings on the coming kingdom of our father David!

Ss PETER & PAUL

Ps 33(34): 2-3. 4-5. 6-7. 8-9.   R.v.5   Alt. R.v.8

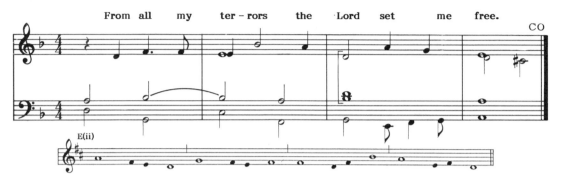

From all my ter-rors the Lord set me free.

1. I will bless the Lord at all times,
   his praise always on my lips;
   in the Lord my soul shall make its boast.
   The humble shall héar and be glad.

2. Glorify the Lord with me.
   Together let us praise his name.
   I sought the Lord and he answered me;
   from all my terrors he sét me free.

3. Look towards him and be radiant;
   let your faces not be abashed.
   This poor man called; the Lord heard him
   and rescued him from áll his distress.

4. The angels of the Lord is encamped
   around those who revere him, to rescue them.
   Taste and see that the Lord is good.
   He is happy who seeks réfuge in him.

Alternative Response

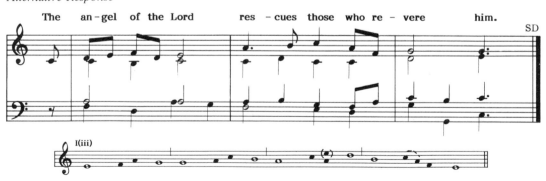

The an-gel of the Lord res-cues those who re-vere him.

Gospel Acclamation

Matthew 16:18

You are Peter and on this rock I will build my Church
And the gates of the underworld can never hold out against it.

THE ASSUMPTION OF THE
BLESSED VIRGIN MARY

Ps 44(45): 10-11. 12, 16.   R.v.10

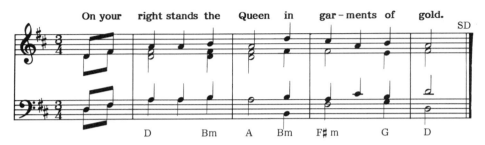

1 The daughters of kings are amóng your loved ones.
   On your right stands the queen in gold of Ophir.
   Listen, O dáughter, give éar to my words:
   forget your own people ánd your fáther's house.

2 So will the king desíre your beauty:
   He is your lord, páy homage to him.
   They are escórted amid gládness and joy;
   they pass within the pálace of the king.

Gospel Acclamation

Mary has been taken up into heaven;
all the choirs of angels are rejoicing.

ALL SAINTS

Ps 23(24): 1-2. 3-4. 5-6.   R.cf.v.6

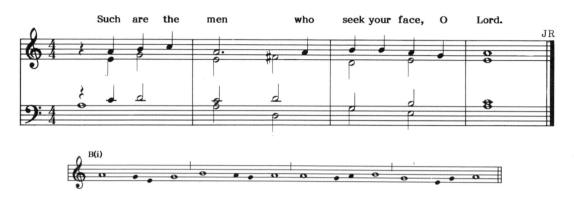

1 The Lord's is the earth <u>and</u> its fullness,
   the world and <u>all</u> its peoples.
   It is he who set it <u>on</u> the seas;
   on the waters he <u>made</u> it firm.

2 Who shall climb the mountain <u>of</u> the Lord?
   Who shall stand in his <u>ho</u>ly place?
   The man with clean hands <u>and</u> pure heart,
   who desires not <u>worth</u>less things.

3 He shall receive blessings <u>from</u> the Lord
   and reward from the <u>God</u> who saves him.
   Sure are the <u>men</u> who seek him,
   seek the face of the <u>God</u> of Jacob.

Gospel Acclamation

Matthew 11:28

Come to me, all you who labour and are <u>over</u>burdened
and I will give you rest, <u>says</u> the Lord.

THE FAITHFUL DEPARTED

Ps 26(27): 1. 4. 7-8. 13-14.   R.v.1   Alt. R.v.13

1   The Lórd is my líght and my hélp;
    whóm shall I féar?
    The Lórd is the strónghold of my lífe;
    before whóm shall I shrínk?

2   There is óne thing I ask of the Lord,
        for thís I lóng,
    to líve in the house of the Lord,
        all the dáys of my lífe,
    to sávour the swéetness of the Lórd,
    to behóld his témple.

3   O Lórd, hear my vóice when I cáll;
    have mércy and ánswer.
    It is your fáce, O Lórd, that I séek;
    híde not your fáce.

4   I am súre I shall sée the Lord's góodness
    in the lánd of the líving.
    Hópe in him, hold fírm and take héart.
    Hópe in the Lórd!

Alternative Psalms: Ps 22(23), page 57; Ps 114(115/6), page 64

Gospel Acclamation   *John 6:39*

It is my Father's will, says the Lord,/
    that I should lose nothing/
    of all that <u>he</u> has given me,
and that I should raise it up on <u>the</u> last day.

MASS FOR THE UNITY OF CHRISTIANS

Ps 121(122): 1-2. 3-4b. 4c-5. 6-7. 8-9.   R.v.1

1 I rejóiced when I héard them sáy:
   'Let us gó to God's hóuse.'
   And nów our féet are stánding
   with your gátes, O Jerúsalem

2 Jerúsalem is búilt as a cíty
   stróngly compáct.
   It is thére that the tríbes go úp,
   the tríbes of the Lórd.

3 For Israel's láw it ís,
   there to práise the Lord's náme.
   Thére were set the thrónes of júdgment
   of the hóuse of Dávid.

4 For the péace of Jerúsalem práy:
   'péace be to your hómes!
   May péace réign in your wálls,
   in your pálaces, péace!'

5 For lóve of my bréthren and fríends
   I say: 'Péace upón you!'
   For lóve of the hóuse of the Lórd
   I will ásk for your góod.

Gospel Acclamation

Gather your Church together, Lord,/
   from the ends of the earth into your kingdom,
for glory and power are yours/
   through Jesus Christ for ever.

MASS FOR PEACE AND JUSTICE

Ps 71(72): 1-2. 3-4. 7-8. 12-13. 17   R.v.7

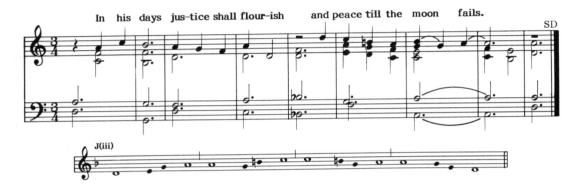

1 O God, give your judgment to the King,
   to a king's son your justice,
   that he may judge your people in justice
   and your poor in right judgment.

2 May the mountains bring forth peace for the people
   and the hills, justice.
   May he defend the poor of the people
   and save the children of the needy.

3 In his days justice shall flourish
   and peace till the moon fails.
   He shall rule from sea to sea,
   from the Great River to earth's bounds.

4 For he shall save the poor when they cry
   and the needy who are helpless.
   He will have pity on the weak
   and save the lives of the poor.

5 May his name be blessed for ever
   and endure like the sun.
   Every tribe shall be blessed in him,
   all nations bless his name.

As an alternative, Psalm 22(23), page 57, may be used.

Gospel Acclamation

Matthew 5:9

Happy the peacemakers,
for they shall be called the sons of God.

NOTES ON SINGING THE PSALMS

Two kinds of psalm-tone are used in *The Responsorial Psalter.*

In the first kind, each line has a long reciting note with an inflection at the end:

(Eii)

My soul,   give praise to the   Lord,   all my being, bless his ho – ly   name.

The change of note is shown in the text by underlinings.

Irregular tones
Normally the inflection has two black notes, but psalm tones D(iii) (e.g. p39) and I(iii) (e.g. p73) have three in some lines. The change of note in these lines is shown by an accent in the text. Sometimes the syllable in question is best sung over two notes rather than one; this happens where the accent coincides with an underlining (e.g. stanza 2 on p39).

Gelineau psalmody
The second kind is usually known as Gelineau psalmody and is based on accents. The note changes two or three times in each line and the psalm is sung more rhythmically:

(L)

I re – joiced when I heard them say,   'Let us   go to God's house.'

The change of note is shown in the text by accents. Most lines (including both of these) have some unaccented syllables before the first main accent. These words are sung to the black note that begins each line. If there are no syllables of this kind, this note is missed out and the line starts with the first white note.

Choosing a Psalm Tone
Under each Response the melody line of a psalm-tone is given, with its reference number. If you wish, you can choose another psalm tone from the Supplement instead, so long as it is from the same group (A, B, C etc).

Gospel Acclamations
The melodies for the Alleluia and the Lenten Gospel Acclamations are also to be found in the Supplement, together with special two-line tones for the verses (printed in the main book for each Mass). Very occasionally the verse is longer than two lines and so the tone will have to be sung twice.
In Lent, the Lectionary prints out an Acclamation refrain for each day, which you will find in the Parish Mass Book or Missal, but you are free to choose another one if you wish.

ACKNOWLEDGEMENTS

Settings headed as follows are the copyright of the composers and are used with permission:

CC	Catherine Christmas	CL	Clare Lee
PD	Philip Duffy	FO'C	Fintan O'Carroll *
SD	Stephen Dean	CO'H	Chris O'Hara
IF	Ian Forrester	BT	Bill Tamblyn
JG	John Glynn	AWd	Anne Ward
MH	Martin Hall		

* Settings by Fintan O'Carroll are from *Responsorial Psalms for Sundays and Major Feasts* edited by Fr. Paul Kenny, © Mrs. Josephine O'Carroll 1983. Published by the Irish Church Music Association/Irish Institute for Pastoral Liturgy, College St. Carlow. All rights reserved. Used with permission.

Settings by the following composers are © Copyright McCrimmon Publishing Co.:

CA	Charmaine Abraham	AGM	A. Gregory Murray, OSB
LA	Liam Affley	JMcC	Joan McCrimmon
TC	Thomas Carroll	FP	Filiberto Polato
LC	Leon Crickmore	JR	John Rombaut
JJ	John Jordan	EWh	Estelle White
PJ	Paschal Jordan	EWc	Eric Welch
AM	Anthony Milner		

The setting of the second response for the 16th Sunday in Ordinary Time, p.57, by Dale Wood, is taken from *ICEL Lectionary Music: Psalms and Alleluia and Gospel Acclamations for the Liturgy of the Word,* © 1982 International Committee on English in the Liturgy, Inc. All rights reserved.

Acknowledgements of the Psalm Tones and Gospel Acclamations may be found in the Supplement.

Text of the psalms from *The Psalms: A New Translation*, translated from the Hebrew by the Grail, © 1963 The Grail (England) and published in Fontana Books, 1963, by William Collins Sons and Company Ltd. Used by permission of A. P. Watt Ltd., 20 John Street, London WC1N 2DL.